Forever You

A Book About Your Soul and Body

Written by Nicole Lataif

Illustrated by Mary Rojas

Pauline
BOOKS & MEDIA
Boston

Library of Congress Cataloging-in-Publication Data

Lataif, Nicole, author.
  Forever you : a book about your soul and body / written by Nicole Lataif ; illustrated by Mary Rojas.
    pages cm
  ISBN-13: 978-0-8198-2708-1
  ISBN-10: 0-8198-2708-8
  1. Soul--Christianity--Juvenile literature. 2. Human body--Religious aspects--Christianity--Juvenile literature. I. Rojas, Mary, illustrator. II. Title.
  BT741.3.L38 2012
  233'.5--dc23
                    2012027316

Illustrated by Mary Rojas

Design by Mary Joseph Peterson, FSP

"P" and PAULINE are registered trademarks of the Daughters of St. Paul.

Copyright © 2012, Nicole Lataif

Published by Pauline Books & Media, 50 Saint Pauls Avenue, Boston, MA 02130-3491

Printed in the U.S.A.

FOYO VSAUSAPEOILL8-22J12-07349 2708-8

www.pauline.org

Pauline Books & Media is the publishing house of the Daughters of St. Paul, an international congregation of women religious serving the Church with the communications media.

1 2 3 4 5 6 7 8 9   16 15 14 13 12

For Grown-ups

How can we show young children that there's more to them than they—or we—can see? *Forever You: A Book About Your Soul and Body* is a resource for Christian faith formation at the most basic level, intended to help you explain to children what being human is all about.

Forever You introduces the idea that each of us is *both* body *and* soul. Foundational concepts of Christian faith such as holiness, salvation, sin, and virtue can only be fully appreciated through an understanding that fully embraces the whole human person.

Forever You lays the foundation for a young child's continued spiritual and human formation. The simple and engaging text encourages imagination and wonder while teaching children basic principles of living our faith in Jesus Christ:

* When we care for our bodies, we also care for our souls;
* We build character through our actions;
* The choices we make matter;
* Our highest purpose is fulfilled by loving God and others.

Additionally, *Forever You* assures children that our souls live on forever, an essential message for a child to hear, especially in moments of grief and loss.

This book was created to help support you in opening a conversation with the children in your life about who they are, how they can love and be loved, and the eternal value of each human person. It is a joy to be human and to reflect on life as God has given it to us. This joy is made even more full when we share it with children!

"Your soul is in all you are and do—soul and body, forever you!"

Your soul is in all you are and do—soul and body, forever you.

Zebras have stripes.
Bunnies hop by.
Leopards have spots.
Birds fly.

You have a soul.

Your soul is your spirit.
It's the life in you that eyes can't see.
Your soul will *always* be.

Your soul gives life to your body.
Use your legs to climb a tree.
Use your hands to bang the drums.
Use your arms to swing a bat.
Use your feet to paddle fast.

Your soul is in your hands when you clap along.
It's in your ears when you hear a song.

It's in your toes when you splash the bath.
It's in your smile when you hug your cat.

Your soul is in all you are and do—soul and body, forever you.

Your soul lets people see you from the inside out.

It's in what you feel:
When you open a present,
When you stamp your feet,
When you win!
When you try again.

Your soul shows through in your hopes:

One more day at the beach,
One more hour of sleep,

One more minute with friends,
One more hug from grandpa.

Your soul is in all you are and do—soul and body, forever you.

Your soul shows through in what you like.
Your mind dreams of ice cream.
Your heart hopes for three scoops.
Your hands reach for the cone.
Your mouth smiles—that was yum!

Your soul shows through when you love.
You love your friends.
You love your family.
You love God.

Your soul is in all you are and do—soul and body, forever you.

Your soul shows through in your special gifts.

Grandma's soul is bright
when she paints on her canvas.

Mama's soul is sweet
when she bakes your favorite treat.

Papa's soul is strong
when he helps you along.

Big sister's soul is calm
when she sings a soft tune.

Little brother's soul is happy
when he makes you a balloon.

Your soul is not made of light, but it warms like the sun.
It is not made of water, but soothes like rain.

It is not made of wind, but sings like a gentle breeze.
It is not made of glass, but reflects what's in your heart.

To: Abby
Love, God

Your soul did not come wrapped in a bow,
Or hidden under a Christmas tree.
It did not wash up in a blue wave,
Or fly down in a jet engine plane.

Your soul came from God when your life began,
Because he wanted to love you forever.

Your soul is in all you are and do—soul and body, forever you.

Everyone is a body with a soul:

Ballet dancers full of charm,
Racecar drivers zooming along,

Friends dressed in their
Sunday best,
All branches of your family,
Everyone—you and me.

Your soul is a gift for safekeeping.
Care for it.
Nourish it.
Protect it.
Watch what you choose to do.
Treat your body with love.

Your soul is for helping.
To those who are sad, offer comfort.
To those who are sick, give care.
To those who are hungry, bring food.
To those who are lonely, be a friend.

Your soul is in all you are and do—soul and body, forever you.

Your soul is for God.
Thank God for his blessings.
Honor God at church.
Praise God with song,
Because God loves you.

Your soul is for heaven,
To one day return to God
And live with the saints,
And the angels,
And your family,
In your forever body,
In your forever home.

Your soul is in all you are and do—soul and body, forever you.

Nicole Lataif

Nicole wrote her first poem at the age of six in an effort to charm her way out of being sent to her room. It didn't work. She finally got out and has been writing ever since. After receiving a bachelor's degree in Rhetorical Studies from Florida Atlantic University, Nicole went on to work for the Archdiocese of Boston. She has also worked in marketing, event planning, and public speaking with other organizations. Nicole is a certified middle school chastity speaker and has taught religious education in Massachusetts and Florida. As a member of the Society of Children's Book Writers and Illustrators, Nicole currently leads a children's picture book critique group in Boston, MA, where she lives.

Keep the conversation going by visiting Nicole's website: www.NicoleLataif.com. There, you'll find resources to help grown-ups teach Christian values to children.

Mary Rojas

Mary Rojas has been working as a freelance illustrator for more than ten years. Her work is joyfully colorful and often whimsical. Mary has illustrated many children's educational and story books for a wide variety of publishers. *Forever You: A Book About Your Soul and Body* is Mary's first Pauline Kids picture book. Mary lives in San Antonio, Texas, with her husband and son.